Panic

PANIC

One Man's Struggle with Anxiety

By Harry Floyd

BELLE ISLE BOOKS
www.belleislebooks.com

ISBN: 978-1-9399302-3-1

Library of Congress Control Number: 2014937597

Printed in the United States

Published by

BELLE ISLE BOOKS
www.belleislebooks.com

For my loving parents and sister

Contents

Acknowledgements

My anxious mind made this book possible. It would never have been written had I not experienced so many episodes of panic and anxiety.

Thank you to my friends and family for being incredibly supportive and encouraging during this undertaking. I have been blessed to have such a loving and understanding family. Knowing that they will always be there for me gave me the courage to complete this book. Everyone who has played a part in my life played a part in creating this work. To my many friends, new and old, you have made my life enjoyable enough to take a topic such as anxiety and have fun with it. Writing this book was a true pleasure, and it would not have been possible without friends like you in my life.

I would also like to thank the teachers, professors, and staff of Clermont Elementary School, St. Stephen's & St. Agnes School, and Virginia Commonwealth University for training me to reflect on this subject matter in such depth. Without your efforts I would never have been able to articulate the feelings expressed in this work.

A tremendous thank you to everyone at Brandylane Publishers and Belle Isle Books who played a key role in making this book happen. You all have brought the words of a first-time author to light. I will always be grateful to you.

My intention is to encourage understanding and openness surrounding a topic that many people encounter. It is my sincerest hope that every reader will take something of value away from this book.

Enjoy.

Introduction

The lecture hall was packed when I walked in. I headed for the front of the room and looked around as I took my seat. I recognized no one immediately. The first days of anything, especially school, have typically been filled with anxiety for me. In the massive lecture hall, I dreaded having to introduce myself to well over a hundred students. I could feel my anticipation build, knowing with each and every introduction that I was one student closer to my turn. This day, however, was different. As Dr. Perdue introduced the course, I began to feel at home. I had found a subject that not only addressed my academic interests, but also my personal growth.

I sat back, relieved, and prepared myself for the semester.

It was a brand new class, in a brand new semester, with a brand new professor. At the time, I didn't know that I would go on to take many courses with Dr. Perdue as I redirected my studies over the following years.

He began the class with a statement he would go on to to repeat at the start of every session: "People want happiness and don't want suffering." The statement resonated with me. Its simplicity was beautiful. It sounds like a fairly obvious observation, but it's a message that may get lost from time to time in our many daily interactions. Perdue seemed keen on reminding us of it at every single class, just in case we had forgotten. I later learned that Perdue would begin every single class I took on the subject of Buddhism with another simple yet profound statement. It reached the point that we could anticipate when he would utter the words, and we often attempted to beat him to it.

Another popular lead he used over the years was, "Having been born as we have, we now face death." This also stuck with me. These two statements emphasized two key points:

1 Life is a struggle and search to find happiness
and
2 Life is impermanent

The main suffering I have identified in my life has been related to my internal struggle with anxiety, panic attacks, and the resulting stress these have caused. But each person has his or her own struggle to go through. A comforting thought occurred to me as I was sitting in that lecture hall years ago: despite our differences in suffering, everyone is searching for happiness in one way or another.

Life will not last forever. Like everything else, it is impermanent. But in our lifetime we all seek to take advantage of the time we have and hope to find more happiness than suffering in the end.

At times, anxiety has crippled me to the point that I was unable to enjoy what I was doing. When it's at its worst, its grip is tight and hard to break free from. When it's at its best, anxiety is a figure lurking in the back of my mind that I must always acknowledge. I have, however, become determined to take back the control anxiety took from me during all those episodes of panic.

A major revelation I had in my young adult life was that I could do something about my anxiety. I was capable of actively working toward greater happiness in life. It is a simple notion, but it is easy to lose sight of the fact that you can shape the direction of your life.

Anxiety has gotten the best of me in almost every social situation I have encountered. It has overtaken me in all the usual situations people typically find stressful: presentation day at school; a first date; the first day at a new job. But anxiety has overwhelmed me in situations that most people would find relaxing or calming too, during regular family outings, and at dinners with friends. It pops up at both the most familiar and the most unexpected of times. Sometimes it's easy to tell what triggers my anxiety—like when I'm trying hard to make a good first impression on someone. But other times, I can't explain why I get nervous. The anxiety simply rears up, leaving me to deal with it however I can.

Dealing with anxiety is easier now that I am older and more familiar with who I am as a person. My worst reactions to it occurred when I was young. I had no idea what was happening to me on those days I was feeling sick to my stomach. Because of that, I had no idea how to react and deal with it, and even after I'd suffered through a panic attack, I would be afraid that the anxiety would come back at any moment. The anticipation of another attack and the uncertainty of when it would strike made me all the more anxious.

When I was younger, I judged myself for being anxious—which would only increase the stress I felt. Over the years, I found that the more I focused on the negative consequences of my anxiety, the more real they became. Focusing solely on the panic that was to come made that outcome all the more realistic. It is this type of circular thinking that promotes and furthers a negative outlook on the situation. Now, I've learned to let go of those feelings. I realized I had to break free of the cyclical pattern created by judgment and self-doubt.

Through counseling and my own personal reflections on my anxiety, I have come to the conclusion that not every anxiety attack I've experienced has had a patent cause. Sometimes, it simply rears up, with no warning, from some unknown root. In that, my mind reflects the fundamental principle of psychoanalytical theory: that our experience is divided into the conscious and the unconscious. It makes us who we are, but it also keeps us from fully knowing ourselves. I attempt to know and understand my anxiety, but because part of it is unconscious and closed off from me in this way, it is a constant and ongoing process—a process that one must work at his or her entire life. Being an active participant in the process, however, is what matters most.

In recent years, I have become more and more invested in addressing my anxiety. My approach to dealing with the difficulties it poses has progressed for the better, and now comes from a place of understanding. At the end of the day, it's not worth stressing out about what little thing caused me to freak out. Rather, my attention is better focused on finding positive ways of reacting to anxiety so that I can better prepare myself for any future situation.

The aftermath of a panic attack is a significant time for the individual.

How are you going to let this episode affect you?

The answer to such a question is crucial for your future self. A positive answer and reaction can mean you are ready to guide yourself in constructing helpful daily habits to aid you in breaking free from the circular thinking promoting the anxiety.

Looking back, I can now make light of the many rash decisions I made as a result of anxiety. To hide my panic attacks and nausea, I did some strange things that now seem almost comical. I wouldn't take any of it back though, as I believe I'm now more familiar with myself and others going through similar situations, even after all the panicking and vomiting and running around in secret.

I am in no way cured of anxiety—you can't cure yourself of who you are. But I'm finished with the secrecy and lack of openness I once associated with it. At some point, I realized that I couldn't continue such an internal battle with my thoughts and feelings on my own. I had to open up to others who were relatable and who could help put me on the right path. We cannot eliminate anxiety completely, but we can focus on reducing it and reacting to it in positive ways as it comes. To that end, I've tried counseling, meditation, medication, reflection, and numerous behavioral techniques throughout my life. Dealing with anxiety is a constant and ongoing process. Not everything works forever, or even at all, but you find what fits here and there and make it work for you.

It is impossible to stop a panic attack with one swift move. Nowadays, when I feel myself start to panic, I simply take a deep breath, clear my mind, and think ahead. I know that the less I give in to it and get worked up about it, the better off I am.

I'm glad to be past the endless cycle of uneasiness and unknowing that comes with being anxious. If you suffer from anxiety, your story is your own, but I will do my best to offer my story as a guide. Happiness and peace will come if you actively search for it.

5th Grade

Fifth grade began with me vomiting.

There's nothing like starting off a school year being sick at any age, but for eleven-year-old me, this was disastrous. The one day you don't want to be sick—the *first day*—was of course the day I had to get an upset stomach. And at the time, that was all I thought it was. A little bit of nausea, or stomach flu—or maybe something I'd eaten the night before. That was what my family thought too . . . until it continued to happen.

Prior to this time in my life, I have no recollection of feeling anxious. Life had been carefree. It was a jarring experience to suddenly wake up and feel like I didn't know how to handle myself. I was scared and shaken up. I was also so young that I didn't know how to express what was happening to anyone else. I couldn't even put it all together in my own head just yet. So I wrote it off as an illness with lousy timing and went to school anyway, still trembling. There was no way I was missing the first day.

I ended up getting through it just fine, and went back home grateful that I hadn't had a repeat performance on the shoes of my new teacher or any of my friends—or my own. I went to bed feeling better, thinking it had been a fluke, grateful that my illness was seemingly brief.

The next morning, I awoke—and puked again.

These bouts of illness didn't occur every single day. But for weeks after I started school, I often woke up feeling anxious and sick to my stomach. Back then, the only way for me to relieve such an awful feeling was to throw up—at least, that was my rationale at the time.

My morning routine was pretty consistent—

1. Wake up;
2. Determine if I was or wasn't nauseous;
3. Hop in the shower;
4. And—if nauseous—puke.

"Puke" may not even be the best word to describe the act, because I usually didn't have much to throw up at that hour of the day. There was nothing in my stomach when I first got out of bed, so I would typically just dry heave, flattening my hands against the cool white tile and hoping for the panic and nausea to subside.

It was a ridiculous scene: a little kid, dry heaving his guts out in the shower. While it happened, a million thoughts raced through my head:

Why am I doing this?

What am I worried about?

When will this feeling go away?

Question after question blurred together during the few moments I experienced the sickness.

A couple of times, the vomiting actually did make me feel better. It never wiped my nerves away completely, but it did allow me to check puking off my list of possibilities for the rest of the morning. I now had one less thing to worry about. Though the anxiety sometimes remained, the assurance that I had nothing left to throw up pushed me on through the day. Breakfast was not an option at this hour of the morning, because I couldn't risk putting something in my stomach that wasn't going to stay down. I had learned to deal with feeling anxious by pulling the trigger on getting sick.

It's a relief to find any strategy that helps when you're in an uncomfortable situation. It's a problem, however, when your strategy for handling anxiety is not sustainable and will not help you in the long run.

Looking back, vomiting every morning I felt nauseous wasn't the healthiest plan of action. Vomiting was only a temporary solution. My body would be weak afterward and I wasn't alert the way I'd wanted to be. If I wanted to truly deal with my anxiety, throwing up was not going to help me in the long run. I was young, though, and didn't know any better. So, I rolled with the strategy until a better one came along.

As the year continued, even if I got sick in the morning, I still went to school. You can't stay home sick every day.

Once I settled into my desk and classes began each morning, I would eventually calm down, and the nausea and anxiety would subside. The environment of the classroom allowed me the space I needed to gather myself throughout the morning. Though I knew that I would improve with every passing hour, it was still an internal struggle those first few hours of the day. The anxiety of not knowing how I would feel from hour to hour, or whether I might need to vomit again, weighed heavily on my panicked and racing mind. My concentration level was nowhere near what it should have been for the first few hours of class. I was focused more on trying to keep my composure than taking in the subject of the lessons. Somehow, I was able to maintain my grades.

At the time, I didn't see a root cause of my anxiety. I don't think my family did either. My friends barely noticed what I was going through—in part due to my consistent efforts to hide my illness when I was around them. I was embarrassed to admit what was going on. Anxiety can be an isolating phenomenon. It feels as if you are completely alone in the battle, when in actuality, others around you can help and are even experiencing similar problems. I didn't realize this at such a young age, though. The belief that I would be seen as odd and different filled my mind. So I continued to keep everything to myself. To my friends—actually, to most everyone in my class, since I'd been with the same kids for years—I was just a little quieter in the mornings, a bit more reserved, until I found my energy and really felt normal in the afternoon.

I could hide the anxiety around most people. My family knew about some of what was happening, but even they didn't realize the full extent of what I was experiencing. No little kid is skilled at articulating feelings of anxiety to his or her parents. Instead, I excelled at being embarrassed, puking without anyone knowing, and being super quiet after telling my mom I had a stomachache again and again.

There were, of course, times when it was impossible to

hide how I was feeling from my parents. They were always checking on me, like any parent would do in the morning, making sure I was getting ready for school and that I would be on time. During that year, there were plenty of instances when I wouldn't be ready for school on time because I was feeling anxious or nauseous. Those were the days that worried my mother the most. She would drive me to school whenever I was running late because I had either gotten sick or was worrying about getting sick, and there was no hiding how I was feeling during those car rides. My family knew something was going on. They may not have known exactly what it was, but they knew I felt sick far too often, and that I was the polar opposite of a morning person.

The concern my family showed came from a loving place. Motherly instinct would kick in when my mom saw me struggling in the mornings. My parents wanted my life to be as stress-free as possible. Finally, after several days of driving me to school when I was running late, my parents suggested I talk with our school counselor. I agreed; she was a familiar face. Everyone in my class had known her since the start of elementary school. And despite my desire to hide the truth of my anxiety, my youth made me more inclined to accede to my parents' suggestions. Ultimately, I didn't have much say in the matter, nor did I even think twice about it.

I began seeing the counselor. Now my school days would sometimes begin with me talking to her first thing in the morning. Since I usually felt most uncomfortable and anxious during the earlier periods, talking with the counselor allowed me to wait out the anxiety that would bubble up during those morning hours while I talked things out with her, before I met up with my classmates. We would talk about the internal struggle I went through each morning. Before then, I had kept everything to myself. Sometimes, we wouldn't talk much at all. We would practice different techniques meant to help reduce my anxiety.

One technique we used in those sessions has remained with me to this day. My counselor would ask me to describe a setting that was peaceful and calming to me, and then ask me to try to put myself in that place. This technique was meant to be an effort to remove myself from my anxiety and the environment that caused it. Stepping outside of the moment is refreshing. For me, the present was often stressful and filled with nervousness that made me want to find the nearest toilet or trashcan so that I could throw up. Temporarily escaping that present allowed me to put the situation into perspective. Realizing that the moment had simply overwhelmed me was important. Being able to temporarily remove myself from the situation, even mentally, showed me, even in the midst of my worst moments, that stress and anxiety wasn't all there was, no matter how overcome by it I might feel.

Even now, when I am anxious, I still imagine a peaceful setting far from the bonds of my anxiety, tension, and others' judgment. Looking back, my fifth-grade attempts to escape to a place of peace were really my first go at more focused meditation, which I've turned toward in recent years to calm my nerves.

Later on in the school year, the anxiety attacks subsided,

and eventually it was rare that I woke up feeling nauseous unless I was actually sick. I got right back into the swing of things, and enjoyed getting up to go see my friends at school. The school year ended; I moved up into the sixth grade, which meant a new setting, new classes, and new teachers. And just when I thought I was out of the woods, I was horrified to notice a pattern beginning to form: With the start of sixth grade, I was back in the shower, dry heaving against the tile again. Each start to a new school year brought with it fresh feelings of anxiety. The emotions would resurface over and over no matter the year, and no matter the school, classes, teachers, or set of classmates.

As I got older, I began to learn more about my anxiety and my body's somatic reaction to my feelings. I could pick up on developing patterns and could almost predict exactly when I would get sick or feel anxious. When I did, I'd follow through with the next part of the pattern: taking steps to hide my feelings from those around me. Since I was steadily becoming older and a bit more independent, I was increasingly able to better disguise my anxiety. My parents stopped questioning me as much, and my friends were definitely in the dark about it. I had become a master of hiding my illness from the world. But inside myself, I was still panicking. I knew I needed to help myself stop it, not just hide it—and to do that, I knew I needed to identify the cause of my anxiety and panic attacks.

Time to Perform

As I grew older and more capable of assessing my own feelings, I became more aware of the causes of my anxiety. I began to be able to recognize situations when my anxiety was likely to rear its head. By the eighth grade, I had clearly identified at least one trigger that would lead inevitably to a panic attack. It was a trigger many others can relate to—performing in front of others, and all the pressures that come with it.

Some weeks after I came to this realization, we had to give presentations in my morning English class. We had been studying poetry for the past few weeks, and everyone had been made to choose a poem to memorize and recite to the class. With the knowledge that this was likely to trigger a panic attack, I had learned to over-prepare for situations that required me to perform in front of a group. I walked into class thinking that no matter how sick I felt at the time, if I knew every little word of the poem I was to recite inside and out, I could make it through the performance just fine.

But in the end, simply knowing that I *could* get through the poem wasn't enough. It might not happen. My sickness was distracting; it might undermine my performance. Feeling my typical morning anxiety, and on top of that, knowing that I would soon have to recite a poem in front of the entire class, I started to panic.

Excusing myself to use the bathroom abruptly and awkwardly, I bolted from the classroom, barely waiting for the teacher to give me permission to leave. I ran to the nearest bathroom stall that I could find and proceeded to vomit. Luckily, the bathroom was right down the hall, and there was no one else in there to hear me getting sick—even though that wouldn't have stopped me at this point. I was puking regardless of who was around.

After splashing some water on my face, rinsing out my mouth, and standing briefly in front of the mirror, attempting to pump myself up by repeating positive little phrases in my head, I returned to class to recite a perfect rendition of Edgar Allan Poe's "Annabel Lee."

Incidents like these were commonplace for me throughout middle and high school. I would be terribly anxious in the morning as I worried about something important I had to do, like give a presentation or participate in an athletic event, and at the end of the day, I would make it through the situation just fine—or at least, I would make it through and then feel at ease again. I would still force myself to throw up, or freak out and have a sweating fit, on occasion. These things would sometimes happen regardless of whether I thought that I would make it through the situation.

In middle school, I began to run cross country, and I continued this throughout high school. Though I played other team sports while growing up, running gave me a chance to indulge a little more in my introverted side while still being a part of a team. I enjoyed it. My teammates were my friends, and my coaches taught me a lot about running and how I could use it to help myself in life.

As much as I enjoyed running, however, I still dreaded the anxiety that came with knowing it was a race day. It was the same type of feeling I'd had before reciting a poem in front of the class.

We had to take a bus to many of our races. If we had a meet on Saturday, we'd congregate at school in the early morning and take a two-hour bus ride to some private school in the country that had enough land to accommodate a five-kilometer race. Most people were quiet or getting hyped listening to music on their iPods. During most of those morning bus rides, I would also sit listening to music—while thinking about how much I didn't want to throw up.

Of course, when you have to run a race of any kind, you can't fill up your stomach too much prior to the race. Luckily for me, I was always so nervous that I couldn't put down much food on a race day anyways. If I ate too much, I knew my nerves would just push it right back up and out. I meticulously kept track of the snacks, Gatorade, and water I consumed on those mornings. I might sip a little Gatorade or nibble on a granola bar because I needed something in my stomach, but I knew that I couldn't push it too far.

Weekday races that took place in the city or near our school found me in a similar situation. I couldn't eat much for lunch since I had to run hours later, but even if I could have, I would have been too nervous to eat. The school day provided bits of distraction from time to time on race day, but often I couldn't concentrate in class. I was too focused on feeling anxious and wondering if I was going to make it to the race without puking beforehand.

Despite everything, no matter how nervous I was, I never missed a race. The anxiety was never bad enough to keep me from competing. This is an important point to emphasize because anxiety has the ability to prevent you from doing what you love. I liked running too much to let my nerves get the best of me in this instance. All I had to do was get to the starting line—if I could make it there, I knew everything would be okay. The time before that starting gun was fired was for getting nervous and freaking out. Once the race began, all I cared about was running my heart out.

A little bout with nerves is always good before a big competition or performance. It keeps you fresh and on your toes, keeps an edge about you. A big case of nerves, however, results in your body not keeping down enough fluids or food for the energy you need. Throwing up takes a lot out of you. I did have races in which I found that perfect balance—races when I didn't throw up beforehand and was able to hang on to that extra bit of energy.

Despite all of the nerves on race days, cross country was an awesome experience for me. Competing with my friends and students from rival schools was fun. Doing well and improving my personal best times was rewarding. I got nervous on race days, but every other day of the week was reserved for practice—anything from a distance run to a hill workout. No matter what practice consisted of, I could be alone with my thoughts during those few hours of the day. These were sacred hours for me during a time when I spent many hours each day anxiously anticipating and freaking out about what was going on in my life. Running taught me to clear my mind and focus on enjoying and doing well at what I was doing in the moment.

Team sports were another story.

I couldn't be alone then, like I was when I was running. Other people were actively depending on me, and I had to interact with them. I couldn't simply let go and think on my own. It was an entirely different situation, one that led me to more than a few problems when I was on the baseball team in high school.

One particular occasion was due to a mixture of both nerves and . . . too much Five Guys. In that semester's class on human sexuality, there were only five of us boys, since the girls had their own, separate class. We were a ridiculous bunch, yet we kept it together enough in class to earn a trip to Five Guys, a nearby burger joint, for lunch one day. Five Guys was deemed particularly appropriate, as there were five of us. I, like the rest of the group, proceeded to scarf down two cheeseburger patties and a bag of fries that had been packed and overflowing to the point that when we poured them out, we couldn't see the table beneath them.

My friend from the baseball team, Tommy, was in the class with me. We joked about how we'd be feeling this later before the game, but that didn't stop us. We had to indulge—after all, the food was delicious. Then game time arrived.

Our opponents were a rival school, and we knew it would be a close game. Besides the massive amount of food

I had in my stomach, I was full of nerves. I'd be starting at catcher and would play a crucial role in the game.

Despite my nerves, warm-ups went well.

No puke yet.

Then it was time to take the field: me behind the plate, and, coincidentally, Tommy on the mound. My friends jogged out to take their positions, but I hesitated. I knew it was coming. There was too much burger and I was too nervous to deal with this full stomach of grease on top of all the pressure. The meal had been a poor choice on my part for a game day. Our dugout had a tree behind it that was my nearest refuge. I littered the base of it with vomit, grabbed a water bottle, washed my mouth out, and was good to go. The tree concealed me from my teammates on the field, but not from the bleachers and the friends and family watching. I couldn't think about that, though. It didn't matter who had witnessed the act; it was time to start the game. We won that day and I made it through the whole game playing my heart out . . . on a much lighter stomach.

During this time of my life, when friends or family asked if I was okay or why I was nervous, I gave them excuses. I'd say that I was nervous for the game, which was true, or that something wasn't sitting right with my stomach, which was also true at times. I would never go into specifics, and those answers seemed to suffice.

My primary concern was always making it through whatever task or event I was engaged in, and once it was over, I wanted nothing to do with reflecting on the anxiety that had appeared before. On days when I was nervous, but forced to be around my peers, I felt obliged to fit in. If we were out getting lunch, I couldn't just sit there and not eat. The last thing I wanted was to hear questions about why I wasn't eating. Answering such a question would only introduce a conversation about my nervousness, which I wasn't ready to get into with anyone.

I wish I knew how many times I've vomited in my life. I know that the number is high. The majority of these incidents were not due to the flu or food poisoning, but were a result of me being nervous and panicked to the point that my body didn't know what else to do.

I find my anxiety is worst when I am anticipating what might occur. These examples of times in which I was called upon to perform were events I had known about ahead of time. I would build them up in my head to the point that I was afraid of failing. I've never been anxious about the prospect of doing *well* at something. It's not scary to know that an event will unfold perfectly, without any hitches. The anxiety always arrives as a result of creating a sense of doubt—*Will I get sick in the middle of this? Maybe I'm not fully prepared. I don't think I can do this.* These were the kind of thoughts that crept into my mind silently as I sat waiting to recite my poem in English class, as I thought about the competition on a big game day, or as I nervously listened to music on a long bus ride to a meet. These thoughts planted the seeds that caused me to panic.

There's nothing scary about knowing exactly what is going to happen in a given situation. That's just normal, everyday life, unfolding as it should, in a relatively uneventful manner. And nine times out of ten, life goes on without any problems. But I found that I had a tendency to focus on the few instances that went wrong. Focusing on those instances in turn made them seem graver and more important than they actually were in comparison to everything else. Even worse, devoting myself to focusing so much on what had gone wrong, and over-preparing to prevent it from happening again in the next instance, the next presentation, the next event—left me with a negative outlook. I would see what might go wrong so often that I would begin to think failure was actually the most likely scenario, when statistically there was only a small chance that my nightmarish worries would come to pass.

To combat this, I began to create my own mantras: "I have done this a thousand times before." "Everything is going to be fine." "Everyone here is your friend and there's nothing to worry about." "You'll make it through just like last time." And "It'll all be over soon."

Toward the end of high school, my nausea subsided somewhat. It was now far less common than when I was younger. It would still come up every so often—at a school dance, for instance—but who isn't nervous when they're going through puberty and have to deal with crushes and dancing with girls for the first time?

Overall, my situation improved. I had my panic attacks under control and was no longer dealing with bouts of nausea several days out of a week. I felt more confident about tackling each day.

Nevertheless, while the nausea was improving, the

anxiety itself had not gone away. Panic attacks were less frequent, but other habits had formed instead. My anxiety was manifesting itself in ways I had never seen before. I was plucking out hairs all over my body, and wasn't thinking twice about it. The plucking process hurt at first, but that didn't seem to stop me. I adjusted, as I had adjusted to finding a way to vomit and still make it through the day. One anxious habit replaced another, and I was all but unaware that the transition had occurred. It was a relief to not feel sick all the time, but I was going to have to recognize and discover how to deal with this new manifestation of my anxiety.

Trichotillomania

One might think I was in a trance.

I sit awake in bed, staring straight ahead, eyes fixed on nothing in particular. I am unable to focus on my surroundings, unable to concentrate on anything of substance. My thoughts are completely blank. It's as if I'm focusing so much on this one task that I can't spare any time or energy for any other thoughts. My hands do all the busy work. It takes just two fingers to pluck each hair from my eyelashes. Then, on to my eyebrows—one after the other.

I sit, captivated.

The disorder is referred to as trichotillomania, and it appeared in my life near the end of high school. Although the nausea and anxiety still popped up from time to time, for the most part I had developed a new compulsion that surfaced more regularly: plucking out my hairs. One habit—furtively finding places to throw up in secrecy—had transformed into another.

During the summer between high school and college, I had started regularly picking at my eyelashes. I would occasionally transfer my efforts to my eyebrows and facial hair as well, or even other hairs on my legs or head, but my eyelashes were my main targets. I fixated on them. I've been through plenty of stretches in my life when I did not have a single eyelash to speak of.

My fingers obscured my vision while I was plucking. In a way, I think this was the main reason it became a habit. I believed that having my hands over my face shielded me from everything else. The trance-like, thoughtless state I would fall into while plucking was just another part of picking that reinforced my belief. Picking at my eyelashes hid me from everything else that was happening, and anything that could make demands of me or cause me stress—including the anxious thoughts in my head.

Most of the times I would pick my hair out, I was alone doing something stationary like reading a book, watching television, or just lying down trying to fall asleep. When there was nothing else to distract my body, hands, and mind, I was in my most vulnerable state.

For that reason, it was always worst at night.

The anxiety of knowing that you should be sleeping and having no other distraction can only encourage an impulse control disorder like hair pulling. When you're in bed, it's as if you're trapped there with nothing but yourself and your anxiety. Hair pulling relaxed me, but at the same time, the repetitive motion of plucking also acted as a sort of stimulant to me. The more I picked and picked, the harder it became to fall asleep. After one hair came out, I felt the need to move on to the next one. There are tens of thousands of hairs on a human body, so the process had no clear stopping point—which led to me staying up much later than I should have many nights.

Once I started, I was hooked.

Needless to say, this habit has been very distracting, and has disrupted my life quite a bit. It doesn't just take time out of my day; it also distracts my mind. It has brought shame and embarrassment to me at times. It had the ability to interrupt any other behavior or activity I might be enthusiastic about, and command all of my attention. It became an enormous nuisance.

When I was in the thick of a hair pulling session, almost nothing could stop me. Worse still, as time went on, the habit grew, and these "sessions" became more and more common and part of my everyday life.

Eventually, hair pulling became a mindless task that just had to be done—a type of chore. Many times, I sat and plucked every single eyelash out in one session. I would sit on the couch for minutes, or if I had nowhere to be, even hours—yet from my perspective, the minutes would fly by. So much time was lost to the habit. When I no longer had eyelashes to pluck, I would move on to my eyebrows, and even my legs, though plucking those hairs hurt a little more so I wouldn't choose them as often. I've wasted entire days sitting and plucking hairs from my face, from my ankles, from my arms—no space on my body was safe from the disorder.

A session begins when I recognize the anxiety and urge to pluck, and once it's over, there is an overwhelming sense of relief. Pulling out each individual hair may hurt at first, but eventually it becomes a relief, even a release, to feel the hairs come out. There is a type of build-up, an anxious excitement of sorts before I get a hair out, and then, an overwhelming sense of relief when it was finally plucked free—like the relief one might feel in scratching off a peeling scab, or removing a hangnail. Knowing that the release of the hair brings with it a certain degree of relief, accomplishment, and even pleasure is enough to distract me and keep me at it. After a while, it doesn't hurt at all.

That isn't to say there are no negative consequences. Be it no eyelashes, no eyebrows, or maybe a chunk of random hair missing on my leg or arm, the result is never something that I want. It's never aesthetically pleasing to see what I have done.

Nevertheless, for a while, I did nothing about it. Making myself aesthetically unpleasing alone wasn't a strong enough consequence to outweigh the relief I felt during a hair-pulling session. And my behavior seemed to reduce my anxiety. The relief was addictive. As a result, I kept plucking—and I hid the behavior from everyone, just as I had hidden my anxiety and episodes of nausea. This went on sporadically for years, and it wasn't until a family dinner one night in high school that I had to admit what I'd been doing to my family—and myself.

When I arrived at my house that evening, everything seemed normal—except for two things. First, my sister was coming home from college that night. Second—I'd recently picked out all of my eyelashes. There wasn't a single hair left.

Probably because she hadn't seen me in a while, my sister was the one to notice that my eyelids were completely bare of lashes. Her initial reaction was one of surprise and curiosity. Sitting directly to my right, she leaned in and observed me up close. I began to panic as my parents started to question what was going on, while my sister continued to examine my face.

I don't think anyone at the table was really prepared for such a topic to come up. Like any loving mother, mine worried about me and panicked about what I was doing to myself. No one in my family knew anything about hair pulling. Their initial reaction was bewilderment, and they asked me to stop. They thought I was damaging my eyes, and were taken aback by my actions—probably because trichotillomania just isn't very common. They'd never heard of it before. It was something strange and unfamiliar.

Society idealizes "normal," and my habit was definitely not that. The pressure placed on me to be normal and cease my habit only heightened my anxiety even more.

I just wanted the attention deflected away from me. I certainly wasn't going to tell anyone that I was picking hair from other parts of my body at the time either. All I wanted was for the conversation to be dropped. *"I'll deal with it,"* I told them.

The anxiety of my youth brought with it plenty of shame and embarrassment, and hair pulling was no different. When I was initially asked about it and asked to break the habit, I was defensive. It's only natural for people to become defensive when interrogated about something that they themselves don't even understand. Pulling my eyelashes had become a normal part of my life, but it was not normal in society's eyes. And when society finally took notice of what I was doing, I got scared. As someone who suffered from anxiety, magnified by pressure, the last thing I wanted was to be the center of attention, especially for such a negative reason. I felt even more stressed knowing that society, and more specifically my family, did not approve.

Initially, my family noticing didn't help a thing. When I went off to college, I would worry about their response to me and the disorder each time my parents came to visit, or when I would go home. *Will I have any eyelashes by the next time I see them?* I wondered. *How much are they going to talk about my hair pulling?* It was as if I was being inspected every time I saw my family. But now, looking back, I'm glad that someone noticed my habit. In the long run, it helped me to recognize what I was doing and to work toward correcting it.

I began to seek out behavioral techniques aimed at distracting my hands. I wore wristbands, silly bands, rubber bands, even hair ties, on my wrists in an effort to occupy my busy fingers. To this day, I often cover my wrists with accessories, sometimes to distract my hands, and other times because I've simply become accustomed to the behavior. I also make a conscious effort to notice my hands more, viewing them as separate from myself. If they have their own identity, I can observe whether or not they are being productive throughout the day.

Transforming my focus in this way helped to curb the effects of the trichotillomania. As it happens, having part of my focus, however slight, removed from the act of plucking seems to slow my hand. If I absently begin a hair pulling session in the middle of doing something else, like reading a book or watching a movie, the effects aren't as drastic. I'm also distracted from plucking when I know I have somewhere to be—that way, I can't waste the day plucking hairs. I know I have to stop and leave, and the external pressure is enough to force me to follow through.

Despite the great effort I had to go to in order to curb my habit, I didn't think of my hair pulling as a manifestation of a disorder for quite a while. Sometimes, the difference between what constitutes a habit and a disorder is unclear. The line is often blurred. I had explored the fact that trichotillomania existed as a disorder, but my family and friends weren't aware of it, and I didn't tell them about it. I had hoped it would resolve itself on its own. The small behavioral techniques I used to try to distract my hands had worked to a certain extent, and might do the job for some people. But I realized that I needed more. Looking at the behavior as simply a bad habit that I needed to stop was not helping the situation. The behavior was too prevalent for me to ignore. The hair pulling had deeper implications and was a manifestation of my anxiety that I needed to address in its appropriate context.

I decided to go to the professionals.

Fluoxetine

The brand name for fluoxetine is Prozac.

Most people know it by that name. It's a drug that hit the markets big in the nineties and hasn't stopped since. Typically, Prozac is used to treat depression, but it can also be used to treat other conditions, such as impulse control disorders. I was unfamiliar with how effective the medication was in treating trichotillomania, but at the suggestion of my physician, I decided to give it a try.

Medication is often the next step used to curb a bad habit, after behavioral techniques. I had tried for years to get past my hair pulling on my own, with minimal success. Counseling helped, but it didn't eliminate the problem. Prozac was an outlet for me. It provided me with a legitimate response when my family questioned me about what I was doing to deal with my hair pulling, as it worked around the clock to inhibit my distracting habit. I have to take time out the day to perform other behavioral techniques, but medication is always working.

When it comes to hair pulling, all it takes is one session of picking at an area to bring you back to square one. I may have all of my eyelashes now, but if I got caught up in a trance of picking at them, they would be gone in an instant—weeks, even months of positive behavior, erased.

This is why I decided to give the medication a try—why not? After all, it was doctor recommended, relatively inexpensive, and easy to get if I needed refills.

For something like trichotillomania, my doctor set me on a regimen that began a bit more gradually than that which he might have prescribed for other patients, just to see how I would react to the drug. I began with a simple, low dosage of 10mg a day for several weeks, then moved to 20mg, and then finally to 30mg. These daily doses were deemed appropriate, as I was not seeking treatment for anything beyond trichotillomania. The primary goal in using medication to help with my disorder was to get me to a point where my behavior was not controlled by my impulse to pluck my hairs.

Another main goal in the process was to establish a state of being that I was comfortable in while on medication. Everyone has a comfortable state of being that they would call normal, a "resting state" that is obvious only to the individual. It is difficult to describe to another party, but sometimes we know we do not feel normal, yet we can't fully explain why. We're just a tiny bit "off."

The first time I noticed that I didn't feel like myself while on Prozac, I was at work. My senses were heightened, and the smallest things demanded my attention. I felt scatter-brained and became preoccupied by little things, like the wrinkles in my shirt. I felt as though I was observing the world through a new lens.

Nothing major happened at work that day, but I was unable to concentrate as I would have liked to on the tasks at hand. My attention was stolen by the need to adjust to a new state of mind.

Prozac is known to some people for its few instances of negative side effects, especially in young adults, but generally, my experience with the drug was relatively uneventful. At times I might have had a change in mood or a bit of insomnia, but I hadn't attributed that solely to the drug. I knew that all of these so-called side effects are also side effects of life that can happen at any time, for any reason. There will always be times when you don't feel like your normal self. Like any other human being, I've been exposed to my fair share of emotions and mood swings, daily shifts that seem to come and go as they please. These are familiar to anyone. Numerous substances can also alter your mood and state of mind to a point where you do not feel like yourself. I'd experienced some of them before. Many people experience the effects of mood-altering substances every day when they drink their morning coffee, and they soon become accustomed to it.

But that day at work was the first time I had felt "off" while on the medication, and I wondered whether the Prozac might have played a role. From then on, it became more difficult for me to tell the difference between my "typical" reality and my reality on medication. I began to question why I felt the way I did: *Am I in this mood because of the medication? Is my mood heightened because of the medication? Is my mood entirely unrelated to the medication?*

We've all been in a situation where we are anxious or under the weather, and all we want to do is fit in and keep others from noticing how we're feeling. On a normal day, you wake up, feel good, and go about your day without questioning yourself. If you're nervous for some reason, you only have to fake acting normal until the feeling passes. But, if you're feeling off, you are constantly second-guessing the way you act, speak, and move throughout your day.

While I was taking Prozac, I noticed that some days this feeling never passed. It would linger on as though I was in a sort of dream state, and I would second-guess the way I interacted with everyone. I would go to class and wonder if I should talk more or talk less. I would go home and second-guess how I was acting around my girlfriend. I would talk to my parents on the phone and second-guess how I sounded to them. I began to question my actions, how I was walking, and even the delivery of my speech. I felt as though I was hypersensitive to the situations I was placed in, acting quickly and making quirky comments and movements that were abnormal to my personality. I am typically a reserved individual, waiting for others to speak or act first. Prozac, it seemed, changed that—or maybe I was overreacting. I couldn't be sure, and that uncertainty, more than anything, was what worried me.

Did anyone else notice that I was acting differently? I still don't know, and no one may have even cared if I was acting only a tiny bit off. The real stressor for me was the internal monologue, the questioning of myself. There was no end to the process. I could never receive reassurance. I became trapped in this endless, chaotic game of acting out my day while second-guessing my every move.

To counteract these emotions, when I was feeling off, I would begin to consciously try to act normal. This was an odd task, because I began to act in the way I *perceived* as "normal." It was an uncomfortable thing to do, as it required me to consciously decide my every move rather than involuntarily go with the flow of things. But nobody ever mentioned that I was acting strangely, which gave me some peace of mind. Even if the Prozac was influencing me, I was still able to pull off "normal." This was a welcome relief.

Again, I still doubt whether Prozac was the sole cause these instances of me feeling off. I'd had days like this before I started taking medication, and overall, I believe that the benefits of trying the medication outweighed the negatives. Prozac never made me some kind of robot or zombie who just went through the motions of the day. It also never had any drastic and lasting effects on my personality. But there were short periods of time where I felt a little bit off, and I felt that Prozac most likely enhanced these abnormal feelings instead of being the sole cause of them.

This was partly why, after a year or so of taking Prozac, I tried what might have been a risky experiment, one which I don't advocate without first consulting a doctor: I stopped taking the medication. I proceeded without going to my physician for advice. I believed the medication was a starting point to push my behavior in the right direction, and as a naturally curious person, I wanted to compare myself—my thoughts, feelings and actions—on medication to myself without medication.

A few months later, I decided to make an appointment for a check-up and discuss the matter with my doctor. Luckily, everything worked out just fine—but I had run a risk in going about the decision on my own. In my case, a little medication had improved my behavior, but some people rely far more heavily on drugs than others. For someone whose situation requires medication, rather than simple behavioral aids, as a primary treatment for a disorder or medical issue, suddenly removing medication from his or her routine can result in drastic unwanted mood and behavior changes. I was fortunate that my situation didn't require me to take medication in order to get through the day, so removing medication from the equation wasn't as monumental a shift for me as it is for some.

Three months after I stopped taking Prozac, I felt good, and more importantly, I'd begun to change my pattern of hair pulling. This is not to say that I eliminated it completely, because the urge lingered—and at times, it still gets the best of me. But, now I am able to notice and stop myself more often than not when I feel the urge to pick. Realizing what was happening when I first began to pluck was a huge victory, because being aware of what you are doing is the first step in addressing a behavior. The ability to recognize the urge to pluck and the emotions that come with it is invaluable.

In the end, though I did worry about the side effects from time to time, Prozac did contribute positively to improving my behavior. The time I was on medication allowed me to see who I could be without the urge to pull my hair dominating my thoughts and feelings. Adjusting to everyday life without such an impulse was refreshing. After I stopped using the medication, I found that my behaviors had been curbed significantly. I no longer had a frequent, overwhelming desire to pluck. The urge still remained, but it wasn't prevalent enough to get in the way of the rest of my life, and that made it far more manageable.

Habits

L ife is full of patterns.
Human beings, by nature, are creatures of patterns—
of habits. Some habits are good, some are bad, and some are
in the weird grey area between good and bad. For the most
part, the habits we practice can either promote peace and
happiness in our lives, if they are good, or create suffering
for ourselves, if they are bad. Practicing good habits isn't
easy, and most people follow a bit of both good and bad
habits, sometimes even with the awareness that the bad
habit is harming them.

Fortunately, humans are capable of transforming the
patterns of their lives, eliminating or picking up new habits.
Additional good habits in thought and behavior can promote
peace in your life. A bad habit can be changed for the better.
This was the case with my bad habit of hair pulling. It caused
me to suffer, so I made attempts to change it. Though I still
struggle with anxiety and the urge to pluck my hair, working
toward correcting my bad habits has introduced new and
positive behaviors into my life that have in turn become a
part of my daily routine.

Curbing behaviors can be difficult, however, because
people typically resist change. Before I started visiting my
physician and tried Prozac, I had made minor efforts to

address my feelings of anxiety. But it wasn't until I was a young adult and living on my own that I knew a regular and comprehensive approach was needed. It took me being forced to be alone with my behavior, with no one else around to help, for me to do anything about it. In order to maximize my happiness and reduce the suffering that came with my disorder, I knew I finally had to make more dramatic changes in my life. I had to change my pattern of hair pulling, but I wasn't sure how.

Before I took the initiative to address my hair pulling directly, I had continued to act evasively with regard to my disorder. Every time I would see my parents and I had some eyelashes, I would tell them that I was improving. "I haven't been touching them," I'd say. "Hair takes time to grow back. Just wait and see." Unsure about how to deal with the situation, my father and mother would accept the excuse, but keep an eye on me. In an odd way, it was a relief that they only noticed my anxiety when it manifested as hair pulling, and even then, only when it came to my eyelashes. That way, I could avoid discussing anything else that had to do with my anxiety.

Although I didn't feel I could discuss my disorder with my parents at the time, I was beginning to make conscious and regular efforts to adopt new and helpful habits that would reduce my anxiety without them knowing. I hadn't told them, for instance, that I had been seeing a counselor while at college.

While I was in counseling, my therapist and I mainly discussed my history of anxiety and nausea and other topics like school and relationships, my future, and how I felt about those subjects. We worked on my responses to stressful social situations, and the sessions shed a lot of light on my anxiety. I was able to put my anxiety in a healthier, less self-deprecating perspective than my own, and in turn, felt less ashamed about it.

Beginning to feel comfortable rather than embarrassed about these topics was a huge step in the right direction. Previously, I had been ashamed and embarrassed of my "abnormal" anxiety, which led me to hide most instances of it from others. It had been something odd that I dealt with on my own, in secret. It was frustrating enough for me to deal with it—I didn't want the added pressure of others getting upset and worrying about me. But despite my best efforts and the habits I formed to hide my anxiety, I couldn't keep everything a secret. As with my hair pulling, my parents would occasionally observe the signs of me trying to deal with my disorder, and then it would always follow—the worrying, the concern, the fear. The last thing anyone wants to be is a burden, but that was exactly what I felt like—a burden. The embarrassment on my part, and the frustration that my actions created for my family, perpetuated the panicking and anxiety in a never-ending cycle. Removing the shame I felt over what was happening to me brought about great relief.

Nevertheless, it still took several months of counseling before I even brought up the subject of hair pulling. I hadn't seen it as a big deal when placed alongside the rest of my anxiety, and with so many different aspects of my life to discuss in therapy, we didn't always focus on trichotillomania. But I knew that eventually, in order to find peace, I was going to have to change my habits and deal with the disorder directly. I would finally give in to my desire to approach the subject.

Around the same time, I began searching for behavioral techniques that would curb my hair pulling—new, good habits to try to replace the old, bad ones. Every little technique helped, and I tried them all.

Like most people, I always have something that needs to be done, or something that I would simply like to enjoy doing. Some days, however, getting caught up in the non-stop cycle of panicking, pacing, and plucking would cause me to lose sight of how to accomplish what I wanted.

On days that I felt particularly anxious and out of sorts, I took time to stop doing everything and find a place to clear my mind and sit quietly with my thoughts. I was studying Buddhism at the time, and I began incorporating some meditation and use of mantras in order to calm myself. If I was unsure of what to contemplate on in order to regain my focus and comfort in the midst of an anxiety attack, I would simply rest with my eyes closed and think of a Buddhist mantra that has stuck with me for some years.

It became, and still is, my standard subject of focus if I am unsure where to begin meditating. The mantra goes—*om a ra ba dza na dhih* and is pronounced as the following: om ara baza na dee. There is also an emphasis on holding the final sound of *dhih* for as long as possible during certain recitations. The mantra is said to increase your capacity for wisdom and speech every time that it is repeated. It is associated with the wisdom of the Buddhas. In Buddhism, a mantra is meant to strengthen your mind and prepare it for accepting wisdom. Mantras are one of the many preliminary activities a person can perform to better prepare him or herself for greater understanding. Buddhist philosophy states that the more this particular mantra is repeated in a lifetime, the better prepared your mind will be for accepting new ideas and embracing positive behaviors. Mantras can encourage you to change your habits. My mantra, combined with breathing techniques, helps me clear my mind whenever I am flustered.

Of course, it's rare to find a perfect technique, and I encountered difficulties in employing mine on occasion. Sometimes, while I was going about my day, I would find myself distracted and uncomfortable, and stuck in a situation that left me unable to find a private spot to practice my new methods. I couldn't just regularly bolt out of a lecture hall or stop talking to a group of friends to go deal with my anxiety, and I also didn't want to. When I'm talking with friends, I want to hear what they have to say. I wanted to remain focused and attentive, and I wanted to be truly involved in the conversation. But if I was distracted plucking hairs or having anxious, racing thoughts, I couldn't give the people around me the attention they deserved.

I decided to start being proactive and take time in the morning to put the day ahead into perspective. I would prepare myself for any anxiety that might crop up during the day by putting myself in the right frame of mind to deal with it before it began. I began to schedule time in the mornings to be alone with myself and meditate.

Finding a time of day to make such a behavior routine is very beneficial. The power of that behavior is strengthened if you are able to practice it regularly and in a comfortable setting. It is reactive to turn to breathing exercises and meditation in the moment of a panic attack. It is more proactive, however, to turn to these techniques on a regular basis. They will have a greater impact when you call upon them in moments of need if they have become familiar to you beforehand. Preliminary practices are often the most imperative as they prepare you for what is to come. Establishing a routine that fit my daily life allowed me to prepare my mind and body to deal with future instances of anxiety.

I added other techniques to my routine as well. For instance, my intentional habit of wearing bands around my wrists. Rather than plucking out hair after hair, my fingers could spend their time twisting any one of the bands on my wrist.

When I pluck my hairs, I lose focus and become completely distracted from anything else going on. But playing with something did not have the same effect. Distracting my fingers gave me some "busy work" to do while allowing me to keep my mind open to what was happening around me. Plucking my wristbands instead of my hair didn't require my full attention, but best of all, it didn't have a negative result: When I stop playing with the items on my wrist, I still have all the hairs on my face and head. The technique was a positive transformation of a bad habit into a better one, one that didn't cause me harm.

In addition to transforming bad habits into good habits—or at least into habits more neutral and less harmful than hair pulling, thereby reducing my suffering and increasing my happiness—I also attempted to adopt entirely new good habits.

At the suggestion of my therapist, I began writing specifically themed journal entries on a regular basis. Since middle school, I had always carried a notebook around to write in—a journal of sorts. When I was younger, I didn't write in it every day, but I did use it to record my thoughts from time to time.

One spiral-bound notebook in particular was where I wrote down most of my more intimate thoughts and feelings. The black cover is worn now, after almost a decade of being moved from place to place and being buried deep within drawers. The cover reads "5 Subject Notebook," but in reality, the pages inside only discuss one subject—me. It wasn't difficult to take the advice my therapist provided about journaling my thoughts and feelings. It was a process I had become used to in the past. The spiral-bound notebook, however, was a less focused approach than what she was recommending. It was simply a collection of my thoughts, feelings, and poetry— really anything that was on my mind at the time of writing—far less precise than what she was asking me to do. Some of the writings lack context and wouldn't be understood by anyone who got their hands on the notebook, whereas others discuss general emotions that anyone could relate to.

In looking back at these writings, I found that my anxiety was a common theme from an early age. Despite the fact that I wasn't necessarily dealing with my anxiety in an aggressive way while I was a teenager, I was aware of it and documenting my experiences through writing. It wasn't until these therapy sessions in college that my counselor suggested documenting day-to-day activities and feelings related to anxiety. My five-subject notebook was the perfect template to do what she suggested and to continue doing what I had started years ago.

The notebook is evidence that I was indirectly aware of the social pressures that I was feeling. In one entry, titled "Knots," I wrote all about the nausea I experienced before going on a double date in my freshman year of high school, when I was still vomiting before situations for which I was stressed about the quality of my performance and the impression I would have on others.

At that time of Knots, I couldn't drive. Neither could my friend Harrison, who called me up around six one evening to tell me that I was going out with him, a girl he'd recently started dating, and her friend. He didn't ask me if I wanted to go—he just skipped ahead to telling me when and where we were going.

I grew nauseated as he told me the details, but part of me just wanted to be able to go out and have fun. That part ultimately won out, but I knew my anxiety was going to creep up on me at some point. It was just a matter of how much it would make itself known.

Harrison's dad picked me up, with Harrison in the front passenger seat. I slid into the seat directly behind him. We were going to dinner and a movie—the age-old standard. I usually got anxious about meeting new people, especially during a meal. Trying to put food down and enjoy a dinner is impossible when your thoughts are racing and you're worried about making a fool of yourself. But this time, I had an out—since this arrangement was so last minute, I'd eaten already. I could let the others eat, let Harrison dominate the conversation, and chime in when appropriate. All was well in my head—until I looked out the car window and realized we were almost there.

The next thing I knew, the chicken parmesan I'd had about an hour ago was about to make another appearance.

There was no time.

The window was up and it would be too late to roll it down by the time the food came spewing out of my mouth. I let go and just accepted what was happening. Vomit came out and landed on my pants, and on the floor. A bit even flew by Harrison's face in the front seat.

To my surprise, Harrison and his dad reacted calmly. Harrison turned around and very coolly asked, "Chicken parmesan?" The smell was obvious.

I was ready for us to turn around and head home, but that wasn't in the cards. Instead, Harrison and his dad calmed me down by telling me a story of how his older brother once got sick all over the front passenger seat. Needless to say, I was embarrassed and felt bad about the car, but I saw how understanding my friends could be. Instead, we stopped at a

Macy's, and Harrison ran in and purchased me a new pair of pants while I cleaned myself up in the bathroom. Then we went on to dinner and a movie with the girls.

As anxious as I was in those few moments prior to our arrival, the night ended up a success. I even met the girl I would go on to date for the next few years. As the night wore on, I was able to calm down, as was usually the case when I was feeling nauseous and anxious. Harrison kept me calm and picked up the slack, allowing me to gradually become more and more comfortable in the situation. When I got home that night, all I could think of was going out with my friends again.

Jotting down stories like this was therapeutic for me. It always had been. They became something that I could reference when feeling overwhelmed by anxiety. I could show myself that I did in fact survive those situations.

In the same notebook, I also included a list of the happiest moments of my life, in order to remind myself that no matter how bad life gets, no matter how much suffering there is, and no matter how anxious I feel, moments will occur that make my life worthwhile. Suffering may be a constant part of life, but finding happiness in these varied places and moments was a way of overcoming the dejection of everyday suffering. I've never had any intentions of giving up on life, but I believe that when I sat down to make this list, I wanted a little reminder of how enjoyable life can be. Everyone needs that reminder from time to time. In a show of reassuring optimism, I even left room in the notebook to add more happy moments as they occurred.

Interestingly enough, the list of the happiest moments of my life includes many where I recall being extremely anxious. Some of these moments turned out to leave an incredible impression on me, and ultimately had a positive impact on my life. Such moments can show you who you truly are and how far you've come. I overcame nights out in which I vomited but still made it through. I could see myself progress from an anxiety-ridden teen with a mind full of self-doubt to a young adult who had become an active participant in the search for peace of mind. Without reflecting on such moments, I may not have seen them in such a positive light or may have simply missed their impact altogether. We are on the go in our daily lives, and action or forging ahead often dominates our mindsets at the expense of reflection.

In today's fast-paced world, it becomes a challenge to make time to reflect on what is happening in our lives. Such exercise in personal reflection is a positive habit to incorporate into everyday life. Without such reflection, the everyday suffering of life has the ability to get the best of you. Individuals aim for the perfect work-life balance and search for ways to combat job dissatisfaction and "burnout"—a term thrown around in the workplace and by organizational theorists nowadays. Burnout, however, occurs not only in our workplaces but also in our lives outside of work. Our life satisfaction, not our job satisfaction, is the more important of the two. Job satisfaction simply falls under the umbrella of life. Everyone questions life from time to time, and it's helpful to take a step back and remind yourself why you're here.

Reflection ought to be a regular practice, or at least regular enough for us to be comfortable with it. When my therapist asked me to journal about the activities and social outings during which I felt anxious, I was comfortable doing so. The younger me, despite his anxious and panic-ridden idiosyncrasies, was preparing himself for greater and more regular personal reflection. Two founders of modern western philosophy, Socrates and his student Plato, taught us that the unexamined life is not worth living. It is impossible to act on something or make a change for the better if we haven't first reflected on why that change must occur, and therefore, reflection and examination of our daily lives is necessary in order to live a fulfilling life. You will learn more about yourself and how to relate to others and the world around you by sitting down and engaging in some reflection.

Why Panic?

Looking back to my younger days, I wonder: "What is there to be anxious about when you're in grade school?" After all, life is supposed to be carefree and lacks any *real* responsibilities when you're that young! Right?

Initially, it *would* appear that there is nothing to be anxious about when you are a child: Generally, adults take care of you, handing you all the resources you need to survive. But by virtue of living in society, pressures appear: the pressure to interact with classmates, pressures to perform well in school, pressures to behave a certain way.

My thoughts were occupied with these various pressures when I was young. It wasn't a single pressure that I pinpointed as the source of my anxiety.

It was all of them.

Some people panic about the big things in life. Others panic about the little things. I'm one of the latter. Contemplating life, spirituality, love, society, the status quo, or the human condition has never posed a problem for me. In fact, I quite enjoy it, and find that I have the most peace of mind when I contemplate these bigger issues. Such introspection allows me to play the role of observer and tease out solutions to these problems without having to face anyone head-on. It's calming to solve these problems in the safety of my own mind. But those little, commonplace difficulties in life always seem to bother me.

There is so much noise in everyday life. Work, deadlines, keeping up appearances, relationship issues, dealing with authority in its many forms, and even supposedly more relaxed events such as social outings, traveling somewhere I've never been before, or meeting someone new can make me panic. The noise tends to get in the way of the purpose behind what I am doing. Everything feels hurried, which makes it harder for me to step back and think about the purpose of a situation. It's easy to get caught up in a panic, worrying about making that first impression rather than taking time to understand the benefit of such an outing.

Anxiety itself is not rational, in the sense that too much of it can prevent us from living the way we desire. Logically, then, we should discard it—but doing so can prove to be a difficult task, getting in the way of our efforts to find happiness in our daily activities as it crops up again and again.

Anxiety can persist through the existence of falsely negative assumptions we may hold about the outcome of events. Thinking about things going badly, no matter what they are, often allows anxiety to take root. For reasons like this, I've often been nervous about something as supposedly relaxing and simple as going out to dinner with a friend. The nerves that can come from a simple dinner out stem from my thinking that I will not perform well—that, somehow, I won't make it through the dinner—that I may end up outside of the restaurant puking my guts out, unable to return, and as a result, disappointing my friend.

It is normal to want to be a good friend and to want to stay attentive during a night out with someone. That kind of pressure to perform well can create anxiety even in a situation that might appear to be fun and relaxing. When you're going out, you want the night to go well for both you and your friend. This is why the panic ensues.

Placing this over-emphasis and pressure on ourselves to do well can be stressful. At times when our friend simply wants us to relax and have a good time, we create pressure that we don't need. I always want to feel some desire to make a solid impression on others, even if I've known them forever. Sometimes all the pressure I place on myself makes the anxiety worse.

In the end, I've found that most of the dinners I've had with friends have gone just fine. The notion that things will go poorly is a false assumption I now aim to disprove every chance I get. Even if you are anxious about an outing, a positive outlook on the outcome of the outing will help put your mind at ease throughout the night.

Earlier, I talked about the trappings of cyclical thinking. If cyclical thinking has you inclined to foresee negative outcomes, then negative outcomes is all that will be on your mind and all you will produce. For most of the instances in which I recall feelings anxious, I also recall them ending well. I attempt to remind myself of this fact as often as possible. Focusing on the positive outcome of a situation, rather than the anxious anticipation that preceded it, will prepare you to anticipate future events more appropriately.

If we panic because we feel pressure to perform—as in the occasion of a dinner or a presentation—the pressure comes from within ourselves, but it also comes from without, in the form of social pressures. We often lose sight of the larger social pressures that influence our behaviors. Just as we, as individuals, place pressure on ourselves to perform or make a good impression, so does society pressure us to behave in certain ways from time to time.

Anxiety & Society

Society provides us with plenty of opportunities to be anxious.

While studying public administration in graduate school, I came across a scholar named Frederick C. Thayer. He asserted that society has replaced major concepts such as cooperation and sharing with concepts like competition and domination. I believe these concepts have become so ingrained in human beings that we let them influence our own mental states. The ego inside of us and the egoism that persists throughout Western society places an eerie emphasis on social concepts such as competition and domination. Our culture encourages competition, which leads to a sense of intense individualism: When you compete against others, the end result will be a hierarchy of winners and losers. We're taught that it's important to win. This creates a set of strict expectations the individual feels he or she must live up to.

I often find the concept of competition to be at the heart of my anxiety—but not in the way you might think. It wasn't competition in the sense of an athletic competition, or the competitive drive that motivates people to best one another. Instead, I felt there existed competition between my own beliefs and the expectations society placed upon me. Part of my anxiety has come from knowing that I was uncomfortable acting and thinking the way that society wanted me to. I still feel this way in many instances and settings, and it can lead me to worry about all sorts of questions:

Should I be competing with others for a certain place in society?

Why am I competing with myself and having such conflicting feelings about what I am doing?

Different societies and cultures make it seem that their individual society's way of doing things is ideal, and that others should live accordingly. That notion is far too rigid. Even under the influences of society, personal identities should never be sacrificed. Both society and the individual are most healthy when there exists both independence for the individual and a balanced cohesion among the individuals that make up society. The unnecessary stress that is placed upon us and reinforced by society to deal with the little things in life is what really makes me anxious. The media presents us with daily routines that are seen as "ideal," and they often go unquestioned. It is important for you to step back and create your own routine.

We have a tendency to get lost in the noise of daily life. The noise makes me anxious. The noise makes me sick. It makes me vomit and it makes me weak.

How then could such things be good to concern myself with?

I often ask myself this question when I am at my most anxious, as an attempt to establish what is important to me. When I take time to examine what is important to me, I can deduce the best way for me to proceed personally. You too, must find a path that suits your own needs and desires, and finding such a path requires reflection on the topic. Individuals ought to shape society, not the reverse. Individuals must realize that society is manmade and capable of being pushed in any direction. I will never let others decide how I ought to feel about my anxiety. The individual knows best what he or she needs for personal peace of mind. When I am more open-minded and less concerned with the status quo, I am more comfortable with myself. Society should not shape the way you live.

I believe much of my anxiety in life has come as a result of trying to fit into the system and norms that exist in society. Before my stint on Prozac, and before I even began to tackle my anxiety and hair pulling, I was overly concerned with how people perceived me. Not in a vain type of way—I wasn't trying to impress anyone or look *cool* all the time. In fact, I told myself that it didn't matter what people thought, and that I shouldn't worry about it. I did worry, though.

It is one thing to tell yourself that you don't care what other people think of you and yet another to actually believe it. Society and its expectations can change our very perceptions of ourselves, and of society as well.

Yet just as an individual should not allow society to dictate his or her lifestyle, an individual should not allow society or anyone for that matter to dictate his or her perception of reality. Curiosity and a desire to understand myself and the world around me has driven me to connect with my anxiety—to even befriend it in a strange kind of way. It is a part of me, so I feel I should understand it as much as possible.

Much of my understanding has come from sharing my experiences of anxiety with those around me. This has allowed me to grow and change my perspective in ways that I would not have been able to without others' input. Having experienced such positive results, I encourage everyone to be curious of one another and want to seek advice and open dialogue constantly. Exposing ourselves to new ideas and new faces opens us up to infinite possibilities.

Openness

Opening up to others is hard to do, but it pays off in the end.

Openness is a tool you can use to get support and to learn more about your anxiety. However, sometimes being open about topics that are taboo in society intimidates people. If a topic is foreign or strange to someone, he or she will be less inclined to really delve into it unless they are doing so out of pure curiosity.

Nevertheless, my interactions with others on the subject of my anxiety have been, perhaps surprisingly, largely positive. The worst reactions I've encountered to my habit have been expressions of surprise or confusion. Many times, my own family was at a loss for words when I brought up the subject. Ultimately, I believe I felt more comfortable discussing it then they did hearing about it. In fact, the level of comfort that I have with the situation to this day I believe creates uneasiness among people who are not used to dealing with the subject matter in such an open manner.

In the past, my family simply wanted me to stop being stressed and plucking my hair, whereas I have always wanted to understand it in its entirety. Nowadays, my friends and family members participate in reciprocal conversation with me about anxiety, and they are very supportive. If, however, you are unable to find support in those around you, it is completely fine and even encouraged to seek it from others instead. The people you perceive to be closest to you may not be the ones best suited to aid you when it comes to your anxiety. Before I reached a point of openness between myself and the people in my life, I sought support through counseling and from medical professionals. I recommend finding the avenue that you feel contributes the most positively to your life, whatever that avenue may be.

It's frustrating to feel uncomfortable around friends and loved ones—especially when you know that the person you are with would cast no judgment if you expressed feelings of anxiety toward a situation. Knowing this, I have pushed myself to be more upfront about my anxiety as it occurs. I often address anxiety in the moment it's happening, as close to a panic attack as possible. This serves two purposes. First, addressing your feelings while they are happening is a good way of understanding them when they are most vivid. Verbalizing irrational thoughts while you are having them brings them to the forefront, which in turn can help you deal with them and defuse a situation that previously seemed unbearable. Defusing the seemingly unbearable can help lessen the grip that anxiety has on your mind and behavior.

Second, letting others know about your situation can give them the opportunity to help you feel more at ease. Give others the opportunity to help you. This can be accomplished by simply making others aware of what is going on. They may have even had a relatable experience they can share with you. It is for this reason that complete strangers will often talk to one another in the waiting rooms of doctor's offices or before going onstage to perform—because they are both feeling anxious and have the desire to express that feeling of anxiety.

Realizing that your nerves are not out of the ordinary is something that I find refreshing. It is amazing how in an instant I can go from being completely panicked to actually enjoying discussing my anxiety with someone. I have found that laughing at myself is a great way of relieving the isolation that comes with anxiety. A humorous reaction to anxiety can be harm reducing. It takes the control out of the hands of your anxiety and gives it back to you. That is empowering. I laugh with a sense of relief, with the knowledge that others recognize what is happening. I laugh knowing that I should have expressed my feelings of anxiety so much sooner.

When among friends, one should feel comfortable enough to express feelings of anxiety if he or she needs to do so. Since I've had my fair share of nervous nights out, I appreciate hearing others open up about their own experiences.

I can still recall how one of my best friends, whom I'd known since seventh grade, unexpectedly told me about his experiences with anxiety one night when we were both out at dinner. He began discussing how he couldn't put food down when he was nervous about going out. He revealed that there'd been times when he'd tried taking a shot of liquor to calm his nerves before the dinner. We laughed at this, and I shared my own experiences with him. This was a friend with whom I'd shared almost everything, and yet, we'd still had no idea of the extent to which either of us was dealing with anxiety. We discussed medications that he had taken and that I had taken. We were relieved to hear each other's stories. Dialogue like this, that allows you to express your shared feelings, can create a lasting bond and a sense of empathy between you and the other person.

After that night out, I am as comfortable as can be expressing any nerves I may have when around my friend. We can empathize with each other when either one of us discusses feeling anxious with the other.

Verbalizing how you are feeling to yourself is a start. You can hear your thought process out loud and acknowledge that you may be overreacting. But it is easier still to have that third party recognition of the fact that everything is going to be okay—or even that this person whom you know so well is going or has gone through almost the exact same situation. Sharing with others can take away the isolation. No longer are you alone, struggling inside your head to make it through that dinner, or that day at work, or whatever the situation may be. Companionship in your experiences can create a sense of immense relief, which can make future self-discovery easier.

Living more openly and having an open mind is crucial in getting past your problems in life—no matter what they are. When it came to my trichotillomania, I was comforted to find others in similar situations. Many people deal with far worse types of hair pulling. Some choose to shave their heads completely in order to prevent themselves from pulling their hair. Others, like me, become fixated on a particular group of hairs and can't stop plucking until all of them are gone. But, hair pulling wasn't the only thing prompting me to seek evidence of others with similar stories.

My history of anxiety drove me to become more open with the people around me. Along the way, I discovered that many of my close friends deal with their own types of anxiety, and for some of them, it has a massive impact on their daily lives.

I have found that a lot of my relief in life has come at times when I am open about my feelings. Freethinking and the exchange of intellectual curiosity is a major part of life. Real and true discourse can lead to the sharing of ideas and provide people with new and better ways of living. It can help break you free from the control anxiety has over your life.

It is important, now, to note what real and true discourse is. There are many instances of discourse that you will want to avoid. Many people, unlearned on the subject of anxiety, may think they are helping by giving advice that is not actually helpful to someone who has an anxiety disorder. One such example of negative feedback might be simply telling you to stop feeling the way that you are. However, I've found that when a person tells you not to panic, the normal reaction is to do the exact opposite—*panic*. And when a person tells you not to do something and they tell you in a harsh manner, the normal reaction is, again, to feel that you have done something wrong—which incites more panic and only prompts you to continue that behavior.

This feedback is not productive, and only discourages the individual suffering from anxiety.

A helpful approach is one that comes from a place of understanding and empathy, but you should prepare yourself by understanding that not everyone is equipped to respond to you in this manner. Doing so will help you to remove the blame from yourself when you encounter a person who responds harshly to your anxiety.

On the other hand, you may encounter a different problem when you show or tell people about your anxiety: Silence.

Sometimes people won't give feedback, because, knowing themselves to be ignorant when it comes to a particular topic like anxiety disorders, they are afraid to offend or mislead the other person. An issue that goes unaddressed, however, can lead to unwanted and underlying tension down the road. If you encounter this sort of bewildered reaction, remember, again, that such surprise is understandable. And in such an instance, if you can find it within yourself to step up and share with this person, you both may grow for the better.

The best kind of feedback I have experienced has come from a place of compassion. Feedback is not telling someone how you feel, it is communicating with the other person to understand how he or she feels as well. Whenever I've been approached about my anxiety, I've been the most receptive and responsive when the person is motivated by compassion.

I try to apply this philosophy to others in my life as well. I care about those close to me, but I'll intervene in someone else's life only when it seems like the right thing to do. Ultimately, everyone's life is his or her own. No matter how well one describes him or herself, it will always be impossible for anyone else to fully understand.

You have to be comfortable with that. And you have to be comfortable with trying to understand others from that place of compassion.

English writer and thinker Aldous Huxley once wrote that we can "pool information about experiences, but never the experiences themselves." We live in a world of social groups, but ultimately, we process our experiences by ourselves, in our own minds.

Everyone feels that his or her experience is unique, and to some extent, this is true. But every time I've opened up to others about my anxiety, I've found that people could understand what I was going through. I've learned that other people are out there taking on their own anxiety every single day. Doctors must see the same things over and over again as patients come in, stressed out about whatever it is they are going through. It's reassuring to hear someone tell you, calmly and caringly, "We can deal with this." It inspired confidence in me.

Any type of impulse control disorder can feel like an enormous part of the person who is dealing with it. I know that hair pulling and bouts of vomiting have, in some instances, taken over my life and have really defined me at that moment. A habit like mine is so small in comparison to others', though. Many people may feel they can conceal it or deal with it on their own. They may be right, but if not, there is no shame in being open about it and seeking the help of others. Opening up and sharing with yourself and others just might lead to a better relationship with anxiety and stress.

Peace

We all want bliss.

Philosopher Joseph Campbell described bliss as both a spiritual and tangible stage in life that one reaches by following one's own desires. We all want peace of mind, and anxiety is a major obstacle when it comes to finding that peace.

Anxiety and stress are a part of life. And it's true that not only those who suffer from a diagnosed disorder can feel acute anxiety: Almost everyone has, at some point, been anxious to the point of feeling sick. Feeling extremely nervous can be counterproductive, but being a little nervous can be normal—and even good. At times, I can even appreciate my nervousness, because being a little anxious makes me feel that I care about what I am doing. It makes me feel alive. Being anxious about something that might happen means that you're stepping outside of your comfort zone and experiencing the world.

In many ways, for these reasons, anxiety never leaves you. It will always be there, lurking in the background. And that's fine so long as you don't let it control you.

When my anxiety is at its worst, I am often in competition with it. Trying to fight it away will do no good. Taking a mental step back and attempting to understand that the anxiety is a part of me and that I must cooperate with it is a far preferable option to being in total conflict with it.

It's hard to give up so much control in life, but that is what has happened to me—and it's happened for the best. I don't try to control every situation anymore. My mind doesn't race or calculate the million different ways that a given situation might unfold. I live open to whatever may happen, ready to deal with it appropriately when the time comes. This brings me peace.

Any experience, good or bad, can teach you something. I've learned a lot about myself through all of my dealings with anxiety, and I continue to learn. People deal with these issues in a variety of ways and I am just following the path that best suits me. Life becomes rewarding when you conquer anxiety, and even if it pops up every once in a while, knowing that you can roll with it is what matters most.

Your own mindset, worldview, and desires determine whether you find peace or not. Accepting such a truth is frightening and liberating at the same time. Exposing yourself to a new way of thinking beyond the usual trappings of anxiety should make you feel vulnerable. But it is a vulnerability that is refreshing and necessary to feel as you begin to change your daily life.

I've always told myself to not be bothered by what others say about me, but for many years, I never truly took my own advice to heart. Now I'm confident that I follow it. My success in this area is most likely the result of a combination of growing up and maturing into an adult *and* overcoming the worst of my anxiety. Besides learning to cope with anxiety, I've also discovered what really matters to me in life. When you discover who you really are, you are less sensitive to what others say you are. You become confident in your own skin. At the end of the day, you know yourself better than anyone else.

As I've said before, anxiety tends to create a sense of isolation. It can spiral out of control and make you feel as though anxiety is all there is to life. The idea of taking on anxiety and challenging it seems like an uphill battle at first glance. We must, however, find moments in life that define who we are, and more importantly, we must recognize and remember those moments. All anyone wants is to be comfortable and free of stress, but one must make a conscious effort to do so in order to achieve such a state. Trust in one's identity and personal journey is a necessity in life. It ought to create a sense of comfort and confidence in one's own self, rather than a sense of isolation and fear.

While in undergraduate school, I had an English professor who asked us to write a paper on "the sublime." The sublime is that moment of clarity when you discover your bliss. Experiencing the sublime cannot be forced, and one only recognizes it when it is happening. It's difficult to repeat or even describe to anyone else, but you know that it is there. I know that the sublime exists because I have experienced moments in my life that transcend reality and that will stick with me forever. The search for your bliss or the sublime in every event makes life worth living. It can strike at any moment and you don't want to miss it. It makes all the anxiety and embarrassment of life insignificant and shows you that those moments are not what define you. The sublime is what defines you. Searching for peace of mind is what defines you.

As I sit writing, I often notice a strong urge to pull my hair. I believe that the tendency will always be there. It is a part of me. Sometimes I even indulge it when I should not.

Guilty.

I am still often anxious about opening up and showing myself to those who don't know me. I may even get sick a few times in the process.

Guilty again.

But I know that I must do it.

I must continue to challenge myself, because living in a secluded reality, trapped by anxiety, is not truly living. It is more like a prison that one must break out of. It is a scary thing to put yourself out there for the world to see, but fear cannot prevent you from doing so. I may get a little sick or pluck a few hairs along the way, but the end result of opening myself up to the world is more important than losing a hair or two and feeling a bit anxious.

It is only by breaking out of this prison that we may proceed to the next step—for although Buddhism has shown me that we must attempt to fully understand our own minds, it has also shown me that the journey does not stop there. Discovering your personal identity is not the end game. With a proper understanding of one's self and one's own mind, you may begin to influence the world around you. You can start to understand and share with others. It is important to be comfortable alone with oneself, but also to be able to at least attempt to empathize with and understand what others are going through. And it is then—united— that change, both personal and social, can come.

I never thought I would be where I am today. It would've been easy to get lost in the anxious and isolated existence created by my panic. I succeeded in the place where I first became aware of my anxiety—school. I enjoy meeting new friends and becoming closer to the ones I already have. At one time, a simple introduction with a new person was a struggle. Now I am more curious than ever. I still have anxiety, of course, but it is the anxiety that comes with the thrill of experiencing life.

I challenge others to follow the path of openness. Reflect on your internal struggles and feelings. Open up to yourself and to the world around you. Observe your reactions to anxiety and seek to understand them.

Get to know yourself, and remember that we want to know you, too.

References Used

Management Skills: *A Jossey-Bass Reader*. San Francisco: Sage Publications, 2005.

Box, Richard C. *Making a Difference: Progressive Values in Public Administration*. Armonk: M.E. Sharpe Inc., 2008.

Campbell, Joseph. *Joseph Campbell and the Power of Myth with Bill Moyers*. PBS. 1988.

Einstein, Albert, & Seelig, Cal. *Ideas and Opinions*. New York: Three Rivers Press, 1982.

Freud, Sigmund. *The Ego and the Id*. Seattle: Pacific Publishing Studio, 2010.

Gyatso, Tenzin & Hopkins, Jeffrey. *How to Practice The Way to a Meaningful Life*. New York: Atria Books, 2002.

Huxley, Aldous. *The Doors of Perception & Heaven and Hell*. New York: HarperCollins Publishers, 1954.

Perdue, Daniel E. *Debate: In Tibetan Buddhism.* Ithaca: Snow Lion Publications, 1992.

Perdue, Daniel E. "Human Spirituality" (course pack for Religious Studies 108-001 and 002, Virginia Commonwealth University, 2008).

Perdue, Daniel E. "Seminar in Mahayana Buddhism" (Course Pack for Religious Studies 490-901, Virginia Commonwealth University, 2010).

Thayer, Frederick C. *An End to Hierarchy & Competition: Administration in the Post-Affluent World.* New York: Franklin Watts, 1981.

Tsering, Geshe Tashi. *Buddhist Psychology.* Somerville: Wisdom Publications, 2006.